these
FORTY DAYS

these FORTY DAYS

Lenten Exercises by
Rev. John P. Henry

AVE MARIA PRESS Notre Dame, IN 46556

International Standard Book Number: 0-87793-377-4
Library of Congress Catalog Card Number: 87-73061
Printed and bound in the United States of America.

Introduction

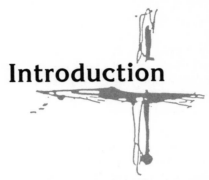

Lent should bring us to stand before God on our own two feet. We meet God and we meet ourselves. The weeks of Lent are not a time for fluff, for shallow prayer or vague dreams of holiness. They are a time for change in the depths of one's spirit. The task is so serious that when Lent has ended one's life can never be the same again.

The Lenten experience leads to a personal renewal of baptismal vows in the Easter liturgy. The 40 days of retreat focus on the renewal of faith commitment as a culmination of the process of conversion. To make this public renewal lightly would be to mock God. We must profess our faith with the utmost seriousness.

These Forty Days is designed to move and guide the retreatant to that moment of faith profession. This retreat manual can be a companion during the Lenten journey to God, especially by those who offer daily Mass. This is not a book of meditations or homilies, but rather an aid for those participating in the purpose and process of Lent through prayer and conversion.

This special season of 40 days can be experienced only by those who take their humanity seriously. Since the dawn of creation people have been tempted to escape the limits of their humanity, the reality that they are God's creation. At times humans even attempt the impossible—to act like God, to become gods.

Through the ages those who accept their humanity and seek to find their Creator have ventured into the isolation of a desert. They enter the silence and the darkness where God can be found and experienced. Moses led Abraham's descendants through the desert of the Sinai, where they discovered themselves as a people and established a solemn covenant with God. Lent demands that we go to the desert and experience our capacity to discover God. Ultimately it will result in our personal participation in the work of redemption, the death and resurrection of Christ.

The 40 days of Lent unite us with the Lord in his own desert experience. In his public ministry he revealed the Good News of his Father's love and God's offer of compassionate pardon for sin. Before he began this ministry, however, Jesus journeyed into the desert with the flesh he had assumed. It was an experience of human loneliness, confusion, risk, hunger and even temptation. During his 40 days in that wilderness he felt the heat by day, the cold by night and the sand constantly blowing in his face, yet he had to go there in order to meet his Father in a profound way.

Lent is meant to be a desert experience for the person who truly seeks God's will and his personal love. It should be viewed as a true desert, a place where a person is alone and cannot escape himself or herself. Lent can deteriorate very easily into something abstract and lifeless. Once it becomes non-threatening, the Lenten retreat has been terminated. One has escaped from the desert. Like someone who announces that he or she is going to find the North Pole and then goes for a walk around the block, some people approach the Lenten journey as a mere stroll. If that happens then God will not be encountered.

The retreat of Lent invites us to risk, to experience the mystery of the desert. There we meet God and ourselves in an extraordinarily profound way. In the desert there is no past and no future; there can only be what a contemplative described as "the precious present."

These Forty Days is a simple presentation: a brief commentary on each of the daily scripture readings, a daily retreat focus flowing from God's word, and a word or two for the retreatant to use as a prayer during the course of each day to recall and continue the encounter with God.

The profound change to be made as a result of this retreat will only result from profound prayer. These Lenten exercises enable such prayer. God himself is the retreat master. His word, the scripture readings proclaimed each day of Lent, are the daily retreat conferences. The scripture text should be welcomed as God's voice. The retreatants hear God speak to them personally, individually, at this moment in their existence. Nothing is to be rushed. God's word should gently lead to prayerful reflection and contemplation of God.

As long as we have the scriptures, we do not roam the Lenten desert alone. God himself holds us by the hand with his word, leading and guiding us. The Lenten experience will prove that God is not an illusion.

Ash Wednesday

What Does God Say to Me Today?

(Let the following commentaries direct your reflections on today's scriptures.)

Joel 2:12-18

God summons his people to sincere prayer and repentance, an all-out effort from which no one is excused. Mere ritualistic prayer is unacceptable. More than an external change must be made. A conversion, a complete turnaround of their lives must happen. Any expectation of reconciliation must be based solely on a change in the total conduct of their lives.

Psalm 51:3-6, 12-14, 17

Sin must be recognized as a rebellion against the majesty and holiness of God. Knowing the evil of such rebellion the sinner pleads for mercy and forgiveness. Pardon received is a continuing touch of God's creative hand.

9

1 Corinthians 5:20—6:2

A person who has received the gift of God's grace, life in Christ, must manifest it in the fabric of a Christian life. Now is the time to live that life. Lent offers the opportunity to meet this urgent need for change.

Matthew 6:1-6, 16-18

Acts of piety and penance—prayer, fasting and almsgiving—must be genuine, not hypocritically performed for vain glory.

Today's Retreat Focus

Marked with ashes, I am directed: "Remember that you are dust and to dust you will return." The ashes of the day are only a sign of penance, nothing more. There is nothing magical about them and any superstitious notions must be rejected. An empty ritual, done only for show, does not please God. Receiving ashes brings about no change in the person marked with them. It is a sign of my intention to take seriously my sinfulness and my need for conversion.

Lent's goal is the believer's return to God. It is a time for reconciliation and conversion, for sincerity and for a profound interior change in the depths of one's spirit.

The operative word for Lent is *remember*. It is the time to remember and reflect on the answers to four basic questions of life:

—Where have I come from?

—Why am I here on earth?

—Where am I going when I die?

—How am I going to get there?

I have a need for Lent. I have a need for *this* Lent. Today is a day of decision about the direction and focus of the next 40 days. The decision made today will determine the ultimate result of this Lent for me.

Today's Prayer Focus

REMEMBER

Thursday After Ash Wednesday

What Does God Say to Me Today?

(Let the following commentaries direct your reflections on today's scriptures.)

Deuteronomy 30:15-20

Deuteronomy, one of the most theological books of the Old Testament, deals entirely with the covenant offered by God and a people's acceptance of it.

Called to conversion, the people are invited to make a firm choice, to commit themselves by sacred vow to a binding personal relationship offered by God.

Psalm 1:1-4, 6

God will reward those who do his will. They will be happy, they will be "blessed."

Luke 9:22-25

The difficulty and pain of carrying a cross is a condition for discipleship, a necessity of a life of faith. A cross is the ultimate risk.

Today's Retreat Focus

The challenge of Lent is to "choose life," to choose Jesus. This is the Lenten decision. All other Lenten resolutions flow from this decision.

My understanding of the account of redemption is incomplete unless I know about the empty tomb. I need to share in both the death and resurrection of the Lord. Dying to self and rising to share the glorified life of Jesus is the re-creation that occurred at my baptism. The goal of Lent is to affirm the reality of that re-creation.

To choose Jesus includes choosing the cross. Through the crosses of my life I participate in the redemptive work of Jesus.

Today's Prayer Focus

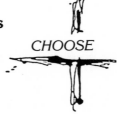

CHOOSE

13

Friday After Ash Wednesday

What Does God Say to Me Today?

(Let the following commentaries direct your reflections on today's scriptures.)

Isaiah 58:1-9

Mere external worship is shallow, ineffective and unacceptable to God, who holds such piety in contempt. Penitential practices should unite people, bringing them to share the taste of the dust from which they have each been created. The self-denial inherent in fulfilling these obligations of justice and charity is the substance of the penance which pleases God and is the source of his blessings.

Psalm 51:3-6, 18-19

God is never satisfied with a gesture, a show of piety, or spiritless prayer formulas.

Matthew 9:14-15

The fasting and penance of Lent are appropriate and necessary in order to be ready for the Lord's final coming.

Today's Retreat Focus

To fulfill religious practices and yet neglect to respond to anyone in need is to be a pious fraud.

Lent is not meant to change God but to change me. Worship is not a way of persuading God to give me what I want.

A Lenten retreat should bring me to total conversion. It is impossible to turn toward God unless in the process of turning around I see my neighbors and respond to their needs with concerned care.

Today's Prayer Focus

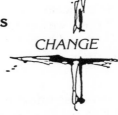

CHANGE

Saturday After Ash Wednesday

What Does God Say to Me Today?

(Let the following commentaries direct your reflections on today's scriptures.)

Isaiah 58:9-14

The prophet Isaiah, as God's spokesman, calls for a spiritual renewal by God's people. He announces that God will bless them and abide with them only if their way of life demonstrates that they are listening to their God and heeding him.

Psalm 86:1-6

A cry to an infinitely compassionate and forgiving God rises from the depths of the spirit in those who recognize their limitations and total dependence on God.

16

Luke 5:27-32

Levi, the tax collector, responds immediately to an invitation from the Lord. When challenged, Jesus explains that he comes to offer the heavenly banquet invitation even to those who are enemies of his Father.

Today's Retreat Focus

"Follow me." The tax collector changed the whole focus and direction of his life in responding to Jesus' invitation. No less is required of me. I must respond with a change of heart and an examination of my personal priorities during the course of this Lenten retreat. Levi left everything in an immediate acceptance of Jesus' offer to join his band of disciples. I must do the same, recognizing that vain gestures and vague promises are not only inadequate but unworthy of the eternal treasure offered by the Lord to those who follow him. Levi was drawn by the presence of Jesus. That same presence must draw me.

Today's Prayer Focus

FOLLOW ME

Monday—First Week of Lent

What Does God Say to Me Today?

(Let the following commentaries direct your reflections on today's scriptures.)

Leviticus 19:1-2, 11-18

This reading is a mere fragment of the 10 chapters in the Book of Leviticus which are known as the Law of Holiness. These chapters are essentially a collection of laws. Their unifying element is the holiness of God, which is the basis for the demanding lists of detailed regulations. God is holy, without fault or blemish, unsurpassable in sanctity, perfect in every way. "I am the Lord." Therefore God has the right to be a lawgiver and his precepts are to be obeyed.

Because God demands it, his special people are to deal with each other charitably and justly. Specific rules of conduct are legislated. The text here concludes with the most celebrated law in Leviticus: "Love your neighbor as yourself."

Psalm 19:8-10, 15

The Law is a clear manifestation of God's will for the conduct of one's life. The psalmist catches us up in a hymn of praise highlighting the characteristics of the Law. This psalm is a profound prayer reaching out for God's favor. The realization that the Law reveals the wonder of God's perfection, wisdom, knowledge, truthfulness and love becomes more and more apparent.

Matthew 25:31-46

The reign of the Law is left behind when the reign of Christian love appears. In the reign of Jesus, people will be judged on those things which they are unaccustomed to consider as duties. Care of others is a duty Christians are bound to fulfill. What they do for others, they do for the Lord.

Today's Retreat Focus

The Old Law command to "love your neighbor as yourself" has been completed by the New Law command of Jesus to love others as you love the Lord. The challenge of the Christian life is seeing Jesus in others and making the appropriate response. The command of the Old Law had to be obeyed because God said: "I am the Lord." The New Law command must be fulfilled because Jesus says: "I am your neighbor."

Today's Prayer Focus

I AM YOUR NEIGHBOR

Tuesday—First Week of Lent

What Does God Say to Me Today?

(Let the following commentaries direct your reflections on today's scriptures.)

Isaiah 55:10-11

People of faith are urged to accept God's word, letting it soak into the fiber of their lives and to become a source of power there, just as rain falling from the heavens soaks the earth and becomes a source of power to produce food.

Psalm 34:4-7, 16-19

Suffering is always part of the lives of the just; they must have faith that God watches over and protects his people.

Matthew 6:7-15

Jesus teaches his disciples how to pray. The focus of the

prayer he teaches is to perceive God as Father. The disciple has a responsibility to search for the Father's will and to respond to it.

Today's Retreat Focus

My Father knows my needs and responds with a Father's care. He is not put in debt to me by an endless babbling of words from a spoiled child, nor should he be viewed as a magician responding to an endless litany of wants.

My sins will be pardoned by God to the degree I forgive others. Much more than a recognition that I *should* forgive is demanded. A mere act of the will to forgive is incomplete. I must forgive from the depths of my spirit, from my "guts," from my total person, from where I am "me." That is how my Father forgives me and how I must pardon every person who has wronged me, scarred my being, attempted and perhaps was successful to a degree in destroying me. Such forgiveness is at the core of the Lenten experience.

Today's Prayer Focus

FORGIVE

Wednesday—First Week of Lent

What Does God Say to Me Today?

(Let the following commentaries direct your reflections on today's scriptures.)

Jonah 3:1-10

Lent began last Wednesday and after a week of the serious business of retreat we need a bit of lightness. The book of Jonah, of which this first reading is a small part, provides that relief. The book makes use of an allegory, a fictional story, to describe the universality and extent of God's mercy. The pagan Ninevites were judged to be unpardonable for their abuse of God's people, but even they are not excluded from his merciful love, his unconditional forgiveness. Jonah himself resisted being the messenger of God's mercy to these Ninevites, even running off in an opposite direction rather than fulfilling his charge from God. The humor of the story is that Jonah's flight ended as, spewed out of the whale, he finds himself in the very place he wanted to avoid. Then he got on with what God wanted him to do in the first place—preaching repentance to the Ninevites. Listen to how the Ninevites heard and responded to this messenger from God.

Psalm 51:3-4, 12-13, 18-19

The contrite sinner yearns for the touch of God's healing and strengthening hand.

Luke 11:29-32

Pagans do not have a covenant with God. They have made no pledge binding themselves to listen for God's word and to do his will. The Ninevites were in that position. Yet they responded positively to the proclamation that God made to them through Jonah, his messenger. If pagans can respond in such total fashion, why shouldn't God's covenant people listen even more closely to what Jesus is saying since he is the very Word Incarnate?

Today's Retreat Focus

The word of God proclaimed by Jonah to the Ninevites was sufficient for them to reform their lives. Jesus, the Word of God, should be sufficient for me. He is the presence of God, proclaiming the love, mercy and will of God to me. I have need of no other sign either to know God or to support my faith response.

The limitations I put on my pardon of others causes me to impute the same limits on God's forgiveness of me. I must confront and prayerfully resolve the issue of total, unconditional mercy and forgiveness—by God to me and by me to those who have harmed me. That double issue is at the heart of a life of faith. That is the work, the blessing of the Lenten experience.

Today's Prayer Focus

JESUS, THE WORD

Thursday—First Week of Lent

What Does God Say to Me Today?

(Let the following commentaries direct your reflections on today's scriptures.)

Esther 14:1, 3-5,12-15

The Book of Esther is a story about God's faithful people in danger of being annihilated. They refuse to conform to the pagan standards and values of the land in which they live in exile. Queen Esther appeals for God's help so that she might protect her kinsmen.

Psalm 138:1-3, 7-8

The grateful psalmist sings a song of thanksgiving to God and pledges continued trust.

26

Matthew: 7:7-12

Jesus encourages his disciples always to seek God's help.

Today's Retreat Focus

A life of faithfulness to God is far from easy, seldom comfortable, never complacent. Nonconformity to a secular society and social system usually results in being misunderstood and often causes persecution. Pressures to conform through compromise often come from structures which comprise my personal world. To compromise is a denial of faith.

Esther saw her responsibility and accepted it with confidence in God's help. So must I.

God is my Father. Do I have faith in the reality that God my Father responds to my efforts to be faithful with his helping care? My confident prayer is a measure of my faith.

Today's Prayer Focus

HELP

Friday—First Week of Lent

What Does God Say to Me Today?

(Let the following commentaries direct your reflections on today's scriptures.)

Ezekiel 18:21-28

God has no desire to condemn the repentant sinner.

Psalm 130:1-8

The psalmist recognizes his guilt and confidently pleads for God's mercy.

Matthew 5:20-26

Jesus speaks here with unbelievable severity. He demonstrates that he has come to complete the Law, including as sinfully unjust attitudes of contempt and expressions of angry passion toward another person. He decrees that reconciliation with another is a sacred priority before fulfilling the duty to worship God.

Today's Retreat Focus

Conversion to God includes conversion to my neighbor. I must be reconciled with others if I am ever to be reconciled with God. Therefore, today I must confront and grapple with deep feelings of anger, prejudice, resentment, rejection of others and revenge. The instances for reconciliation must be specific. Grandiose, general or unidentified resolutions are dreams and wishes. These might provide the consolation of lofty idealism but not the purification of which my sorrow and God's specific forgiveness is made. My offended neighbor is specific. That person is not nameless or faceless, anymore than my feelings of contempt, anger or revenge are impersonal or vague.

Today the psalmist gives me direction for the task I face. "Out of the depths I cry to you, O Lord. . . ." Coming to grips with my need for God's pardon is deeply personal. It is neither an intellectual recognition or a volitional action. It must be experienced in the depths of my spirit. I have to experience my personal inability for any successful self-pardon, although that certainly should follow from the full recognition of God's forgiveness.

I squirm in the pain of desire for God's healing touch, much as I act in the throes of severe physical or emotional pain. That position can also portray the conflict I undergo as I grope and wrestle with the deep pain of forgiving those who have grievously wounded me. The act of total pardon is likewise a task for this day of retreat.

I must cope with my discrimination toward individuals or groups when I am contemptuous because of their race, nationality or social standing. Humor and jokes enjoyed which ridicule people because of these categories is an expression of discrimination. Discrimination is a sin.

Today's Prayer Focus

FORGIVE

Saturday—First Week of Lent

What Does God Say to Me Today?

(Let the following commentaries direct your reflections on today's scriptures.)

Deuteronomy 26:16-19

The bond of covenant pledge entered into by God and his people is expressed by the formula: "I am your God; you are my people." Thereafter God's people are sacred to him.

Psalm 119:1-2, 4-5, 7-8

This psalm is a song of praise about the Law of God and the joys to be found by the person who keeps it.

Matthew 5:43-48

The Father is provident to all persons, both good and bad. The child of God cannot be less. Loving care and acceptance extended to every single person are the distinguishing marks of a child of God and necessary ingredients of a life of faithfulness.

Today's Retreat Focus

The Lord promulgates a new commandment of love in today's gospel text. It is an absolute requirement for those entering the new covenant. The commandments are often viewed as one-sided, severe, negative, oppressive, unbending, threatening and impossible to keep. The word of God today should lead to a different view. The Law is mutually agreed upon, accepted by both parties to the covenant. I am assured of God's acceptance because of my faithfulness in keeping his commandments. This permits me to make today's psalm my prayer.

Today's Prayer Focus

I AM YOUR GOD—YOU ARE MY PEOPLE.

Monday—Second Week of Lent

What Does God Say to Me Today?

(Let the following commentaries direct your reflections on today's scriptures.)

Daniel 9:4-10

As repeated unfaithfulness to the pledges made to God by his people are shamefully recognized, God's patient faithfulness to them is happily recalled.

Psalm 79:8, 9, 11, 13

Conscious of personal need for merciful pardon the sinner appeals to God who is perfectly good.

Luke 6:36-38

Jesus warns his disciples not to judge harshly. He is not speaking of their judging unfairly. Rather, he directs them not to judge with severity. A disciple's capacity to judge generously will be exceeded by God's generosity when it comes to judging that disciple's own faults and merits.

Today's Retreat Focus

I plead with my God for compassionate pardon, to recognize my weakness and to forgive my malice, to pardon my unfaithfulness time after time. A child of the Father, I beg him to show a Father's gentleness, not to judge me as my sins deserve, not to be harsh with me as justice alone might demand.

Today I must come to grips with the measure of severity I bring to my judgment of others, those who have flouted God's laws, but especially those who have harmed and wounded me personally. The measure I measure with will be used by my God in measuring my actions.

Today's Prayer Focus

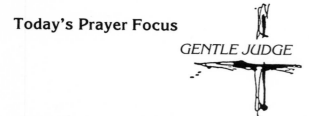

GENTLE JUDGE

Tuesday—Second Week of Lent

What Does God Say to Me Today?

(Let the following commentaries direct your reflections on today's scriptures.)

Isaiah 1:10, 16-20

Sin is intolerable in the presence of God's holiness. Covenant unfaithfulness can be corrected only through the cleansing of repentance and reform. The mere gesture of a superficial ritual is despicable to God and totally unacceptable.

Psalm 50:8-9, 16-17, 21, 23

The psalmist picks up the theme of today's first reading, correcting the insincerity of offering mere external worship which does not involve the mind, will and spirit of the participant.

Matthew 23:1-12

Pharisees and scribes possessed an authority to teach, but the Lord criticizes them for not practicing what they were teaching others. They reveled in the status and honors the title "teacher" warranted, but their fulfillment of that role was vain and sterile, meriting no reward.

Today's Retreat Focus

Unless it is a sincere expression of mind and heart, an actual personal encounter between God and me, any time spent in private prayer or public worship is empty formalism, hypocritical and of little value. A life of faith can never permit deception or insincerity. God will not tolerate a religion without faith. My response of faith cannot consist of posturing, posing or preening.

A retreat task today is to assess the fulfillment of responsibilities designated by titles which are mine. A title should identify a person performing a service—mother, father, pastor, bishop, Christian.

Today's Prayer Focus

SINCERITY

36

Wednesday—Second Week of Lent

What Does God Say to Me Today?

(Let the following commentaries direct your reflections on today's scriptures.)

Jeremiah 18:18-20

Jeremiah is a prophet, God's spokesman, and his divinely directed message is unpalatable to the corrupt leaders of God's people. They hatch a murder plot against him and in the terror of these intrigues Jeremiah calls to God for help. At the same time he pleads for God's care of this covenant people.

Psalm 31:5-6, 14-16

Rescued from the plots of men the psalmist thanks God, affirming his trust in God's continued protection.

Matthew 20:17-28

Jesus predicts his sufferings and crucifixion and foretells his resurrection. The mother of James and John reflects popular messianic expectations of a temporal kingdom in her request to the Lord.

Today's Retreat Focus

The Lord died with a verse of today's psalm on his lips: "Into your hands I commend my spirit." That attitude of the Lord's must be mine. This Lenten retreat should lead me to make that prayer my own in my life of faith.

Zebedee's wife wanted the best for her sons. She wanted them right next to Jesus. That should be the desire and objective not only of every parent of faith, but also of every person of faith regarding his or her own position with the Lord. My life must demonstrate that this is my goal, that I am ready to drink the cup of sacrificing my own comfort, drives, wants and will in order to obtain it.

Today's Prayer Focus

"CAN YOU DRINK OF THE CUP . . . ?"

Thursday—Second Week of Lent

What Does God Say to Me Today?

(Let the following commentaries direct your reflections on today's scriptures.)

Jeremiah 17:5-10

The wise man finds his security in God alone. That wisdom underlies his constant faithfulness to the covenant pledges he has made. Such a person's life is satisfying, peaceful and has the assurance of God's care and reward.

Psalm 1:1-4, 6

The psalmist repeats the thoughts of Jeremiah in the first reading today: By knowing and responding to God's will the person of faith will find happiness and obtain God's blessings.

Luke 16:19-31

The parable of the beggar Lazarus and the rich man carries the message that earthly possessions are to be used responsibly. Comfortable people cannot be indifferent to the agonized cries of the poor.

Today's Retreat Focus

A person of faith is vastly different from a person who merely participates in religious exercises. To be a person of faith I must search out God's will and then do it. I can't be a secularist, putting my confidence in what material things have to offer; nor can I be a ritualist, satisfied with a routine of spiritless, impersonal, empty prayer formulas and pious practices.

Today's Prayer Focus

BE FAITHFUL

Friday—Second Week of Lent

What Does God Say to Me Today?

(Let the following commentaries direct your reflections on today's scriptures.)

Genesis 37:3-4, 12-13, 17-28

Joseph is a chief figure in God's covenant pledge to his people of the Old Testament. The history of Joseph is a dramatic sequence that shows divine providence is not always accomplished by miraculous intervention but usually through an ordinary course of human events. Joseph, the victim of his brothers' jealousy, will ultimately save them and their families from starvation.

Psalm 105:16-21

The psalmist continues the story of Joseph, summarizing his release from prison following his correct interpretation of the king's dream about a forthcoming famine.

Matthew 21:33-43, 45-46

The tension in this parable heightens as the religious leaders are drawn into the dialogue with Jesus and end up condemning themselves.

Today's Retreat Focus

The history of Joseph repeats itself in my life. To live with firm faith in God's continuing care is neither quietism nor fatalism. On this retreat day I see the events of Joseph's life as a demonstration of God's providence. I seek the wisdom to realize that my glory will be achieved when trials have been encountered with the help of a provident God.

The jealousy of Joseph's brothers drives them to do unbelievable things to their brother. In the gospel parable the jealousy of the tenant farmers even brings them to murder the vineyard owner's son.

Today I recall the damage and pain my jealousy has caused, recognize any jealous protection of my possessions, and determine the changes I must make.

Today's Prayer Focus

JEALOUSY

42

Saturday—Second Week of Lent

What Does God Say to Me Today?

(Let the following commentaries direct your reflections on today's scriptures.)

Micah 7:14-15, 18-20

There is a tinge of loneliness in this reading as an unfaithful people recall God's historical care of them and now yearn for his forgiveness and his healing touch.

Psalm 103:1-4, 9-12

A song of gratitude acknowledges the Lord's mercy both past and present.

Luke 15:1-3, 11-32

The good news of divine mercy is taught in the Lord's parable of two sons and their father. The unexpected forgiveness which the younger son receives from his father is total. The heavenly banquet is prepared for the repentant sinner.

Today's Retreat Focus

I must do more than believe that God my Father forgives me. I must have faith in that forgiveness. Today I wrestle with the reality that God loves me with complete compassionate forgiveness of my unfaithfulness to him. Such unconditional total pardon is beyond human expectations. That is the God to whom I can be faithful.

Note this action of the father in the gospel parable: He went out to the older as well as to the younger son. Each of them was unfaithful in his own unique way. Such a love by God my Father cannot be rejected by me, regardless of the son with whom I can identify.

Having drawn far from my Father by unfaithfulness, I timidly turn to him with self-reproach. Now is the time to prepare for my Lenten participation in the sacrament of reconciliation.

Today's Prayer Focus

As far as the east is from the west . . .
has he put our transgressions from him.

(Ps 15:12)

Monday—Third Week of Lent

What Does God Say to Me Today?

(Let the following commentaries direct your reflections on today's scriptures.)

2 Kings 5:1-15

This scripture account has its setting during the time of recurring wars between Israel and Syria. Syria possessed an advanced culture. Medicine, diplomacy and military skill made that nation rich and powerful. The culture was permeated with idolatry and magical ritual. With such a historical setting we can better appreciate the approach of Naaman to Elisha—the use of a diplomatic letter, the violent reaction of Israel's king upon the receipt of the letter, Naaman's expectation of a cure by means of magical formulas, and finally the prescribed ritual to wash seven times.

Psalms 42:1,3; 43:3,4

The psalmist laments his separation from God, and yearns for the experience of worshipping in the temple at Jerusalem, as he pours out an overflowing gratitude to God for his goodness.

Luke 4:24-30

Jesus returns to his home town for a visit. His fellow citizens challenge him to perform miraculous things there but he refuses because of their lack of faith in him.

Today's Retreat Focus

Sin traditionally has been compared to leprosy. Naaman the leper was not directed to do anything extraordinary to bring about his cure. Neither am I! He was asked to have faith. So am I!

A Christian is a threat and an embarrassment to a complacent society just as Jesus was to his fellow citizens of Nazareth. He was rejected because he didn't produce what they wanted. A secular-minded world holds the Christian in the same contempt. This occurs not only when the Christian gives the wrong answers to the obviously simple questions of society, but most especially when the Christian asks the wrong questions of that society.

46

Today's Prayer Focus

TRUSTFUL FAITH

Tuesday—Third Week of Lent

What Does God Say to Me Today?

(Let the following commentaries direct your reflections on today's scriptures.)

Daniel 3:25, 34-43

The Book of Daniel is historical fiction. The sacred writer uses this literary device to teach that God always protects those who are faithful to him.

The text today reveals that in worshipping God repentance has special sacrificial value since it involves a person totally. In repentance a worshipper is both offerer and victim.

Psalm 25:4-9

No one can do God's will unless that will is known. The psalmist pleads here for the divine gifts of wisdom, knowledge and understanding to guide him in the way of God.

Matthew 18:21-35

God's places no limits on his pardon and neither should his disciples measure their pardon of others.

Today's Retreat Focus

To respond with faith is the work and the objective of my Lenten retreat. Forgiveness is an act of faith. The Lenten sacrifice acceptable to God is the sacrifice I make of myself in pardoning the one who has harmed me. This is my way of taking up a cross and following Jesus who forgave even those who brought him to the horror of his own crucifixion. My vows of faithfulness require the constant witness of personal forgiveness. If I believe that I am to proclaim the gospel I must be convinced that it is proclaimed each time I forgive another person.

Today's Prayer Focus

TOTAL PARDON

Wednesday—Third Week of Lent

What Does God Say to Me Today?

(Let the following commentaries direct your reflections on today's scriptures.)

Deuteronomy 4:1, 5-9

God's covenant pledge to the Israelites is fulfilled by their possession of the land of Canaan which they are about to enter. Moses exhorts them in turn to respond with fidelity to their covenant pledge to obey the Law he is about to announce. By their response to the Law they will be responding to the presence of God with them; they will be living with God.

Psalm 147:12-13, 15-16, 19-20

God is praised for his power over nature and his care of his people.

50

Matthew 5:17-19

The Sermon on the Mount introduced by today's gospel proclaims a new revelation. Jesus, a new Moses on a new Mount Sinai, announces that he has come to complete and fulfill the revelation of God's will, care, faithfulness and continuing relationship with his people. The good works of God's people must reflect not merely the fulfillment of legal prescripts but a faithful response to God whose voice is heard, who reveals himself, in every word of scripture.

Today's Retreat Focus

Jesus completed the revelation of God to me not only by what he said but by his personal involvement in the grand finale of divine love, the drama of the Incarnation and Redemption. Nothing else remains for me to know about God's love and desire for me. Jesus perfected the covenant contract through his personal participation in enacting the new covenant.

Today's word of God remotely introduces Jesus as the Servant of God prophesied by Isaiah. He will identify fully with that title in his total acceptance of his Father's will. He will fulfill the role of the Suffering Servant to the point of complete annihilation.

His resurrection will be the manifestation of the acceptance of such faithfulness. He has come to fulfill and complete the Law and the prophets.

I have been brought into that dynamic action through baptismal life. I must be the servant of God by my faithfulness.

Today's Prayer Focus

COVENANT FAITHFULNESS

52

Thursday—Third Week of Lent

What Does God Say to Me Today?

(Let the following commentaries direct your reflections on today's scriptures.)

Jeremiah 7:23-28

The prophet indicts the people for substituting a system of external ritual for the personal, throbbing and vital response which should characterize their worship of God. Religious practices are condemned as hypocritical unless they are an expression of true devotion, adoration, worship and faith.

Psalm 95:1-2, 6-9

God's people are exhorted to praise and worship the Lord who has saved them.

Luke 11:14-23

Luke presents Jesus here as the new Moses, the one in whom God's spirit is present. He is to be accepted as such with total faith. There can be no middle position of faith in the Lord.

Today's Retreat Focus

Today is the mid-point of Lent and appropriately the word of God focuses attention on the choices to be made during this Lenten retreat. It is the time to recognize the divided kingdom of a hardened heart, the areas in my life from which fidelity to the pledges of my baptism covenant have been barred, the places in my life from which God is excluded. This is not the time for theorizing, but for concrete decision-making with God's help.

The scriptures are the revelation of God to me: "Listen to my voice." I must do more than hear the word of God. I must *listen* and listening implies making an appropriate reply.

Today's Prayer Focus

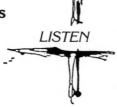

LISTEN

Friday—Third Week of Lent

What Does God Say to Me Today?

(Let the following commentaries direct your reflections on today's scriptures.)

Hosea 14:2-10

In its search for riches and security the northern kingdom of Israel separated itself from Judah, thereby dividing God's people, and had gone so far as to negotiate an alliance with pagan Assyria. As a result of that association pagan worship became part of the life and culture of the Israelites. The prophet Hosea warns them here that such infidelity will only result in their punishment, and calls them to return to God, a faithful lover who will forgive them. This reading is a strong and tender description of God's pardoning love.

Psalm 81:6-11, 14, 17

God's people can rejoice in the wonder of the experience of being freed from the punishment brought on themselves by their infidelity.

Mark 12:28-34

To love God totally is the basic pledge of the covenant upon which all other pledges depend. Jesus unites the command to love God and neighbor into a single moral precept.

Today's Retreat Focus

As the second half of my Lenten retreat commences today, God stresses in his word to me that his fidelity is complete, his love is unrelenting and his forgiveness is total. These realities have been proclaimed already in previous days of my retreat, but today they are blended together for deeper understanding and my faith response. This consideration makes me more aware not only of the dynamics of the covenant but of the dynamics of this retreat as well.

God's love for me demands my personal response of love for him. The vitality of our mutual love is the firm foundation of our mutual covenant. Today I measure my response to the command to love God with my whole heart, soul, mind and strength. My consideration of this command cannot be superficial. Today I confront the reality of my God and the response to be made in my relationship with him.

Today's Prayer Focus

FAITHFULNESS TO GOD AND NEIGHBOR

Saturday—Third Week of Lent

What Does God Say to Me Today?

(Let the following commentaries direct your reflections on today's scriptures.)

Hosea 6:1-6

The prophet Hosea tells the people that dreams of glory are futile as long as they continue their infidelity to God, depending on mere rituals of worship while refusing to obey the commandments. Their repentance is insincere and therefore ineffective, evaporating as quickly as the morning dew. The fundamental demand of God is for people's hearts and wills. Anything else is unacceptable.

Psalm 51:3-4, 18-21

This is a sinner's song of regret, an appeal for God's mercy and a recognition that God wants a change of heart by the sinner if forgiveness is ever to be granted.

58

Luke 18:9-14

Jesus teaches a lesson about humility but even more so he reveals that no one is excluded from the merciful forgiveness of God. The closing sentence of the parable refers to the finality and justice of the Last Judgment.

Today's Retreat Focus

Two men went up to the temple to pray. One did and one didn't. Today I want to identify myself with one of these men. The Pharisee, aware of all the good things he was doing for God, paraded his goodness before himself. He was self-centered and not God-centered. The tax collector, on the other hand, had a sense of the reality of God—his holiness, awesomeness, power, goodness and mercy. He knew that God responded to him not because he was good but because God was good. He prayed well and went home justified. The Pharisee, meanwhile, got no pats on the back from God. He got zero! My prayer must always acknowledge my desperate need for God.

I can consider no one, myself or anyone else, beyond redemption or excluded from God's mercy. I must be a sign to my world of the merciful love and forgiveness of God. That's the folly of Christianity.

Today's Prayer Focus

LORD, BE MERCIFUL

Monday—Fourth Week of Lent

What Does God Say to Me Today?

(Let the following commentaries direct your reflections on today's scriptures.)

Isaiah 65:17-21

This finale of Isaiah's prophecy portrays the image of God's people returning to Jerusalem in triumph. It is a message of hope reminding this exiled people that God does not desire to separate them from himself, to banish them or exterminate them. His relationship with them is not destructive. God loves them and cares for them with tenderness and merciful healing, desiring only to lead them to the peace and joy of his kingdom.

Psalm 30:2, 4-6, 11-13

All are invited by the psalmist to join in a song of thanksgiving to God who brings his concerned care to each and every person.

John 4:43-54

Jesus cures the son of a royal official who puts faith in him.

Today's Retreat Focus

In the first reading from Isaiah today a people as good as dead are pictured entering their holy city of Jerusalem once again. In the gospel I witness a son as good as dead by sickness being cured by Jesus and restored to his father. And the psalm today describes God's care changing weeping into rejoicing and mourning into dancing. That is precisely my delight as I experience God's pardon and anticipate his promise to be in his presence forever when my exile here on earth comes to an end. Today should be an "up" day, a day of hope, in my Lenten retreat experience.

Lent is about baptism and baptism is about death and life—death to self and life in God. Today's scripture readings speak of death and life. These themes are appropriate at this point in my retreat as I continue the task of preparing to renew my baptismal vows, my covenant pledge, at the Easter liturgy.

Today's Prayer Focus

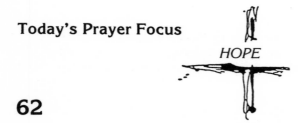

HOPE

Tuesday—Fourth Week of Lent

What Does God Say to Me Today?

(Let the following commentaries direct your reflections on today's scriptures.)

Ezekiel 47:1-9, 12

God is present to his people in a creative, lifegiving way. He frees them from the bondage of exile and brings them once again to occupy the productive land of covenant promise. The prophet here recalls for the exiles their memories of the Temple of Jerusalem where God is present to his people in a special way, pouring forth both temporal and spiritual blessings through his measureless power.

Psalm 46:2-3, 5-6, 7-9

The psalmist sings the song of Zion, a song to God present in the Temple on the hill of Zion in Jerusalem. God's people have nothing to fear because of his protective presence with them.

John 5:1-3, 5-16

By the power of his word Jesus gives health, the fullness of life, to the sick man he has cured at the Pool of Bethesda. With a word Jesus does for the man what the water had been unable to do.

Today's Retreat Focus

God speaks to me today about the water which provided an abundance of food for his people in the land of covenant promise, and a miraculous cure at the Pool of Bethesda for the paralyzed man in the gospel account. The water of my baptism was lifegiving. God became present to me at baptism in a creative way, in a way he was never present to his people in the Temple of Zion. The water of baptism made the arid wilderness called "me" vibrant and fruitful. Something dead to God became alive with God. The Father accepts me as his own because he sees Jesus, whose life I share, in me. The miracle of my baptism transcends the law of nature by the words of Jesus, "I baptize you. . . ," as once his word transcended the law of nature at the Pool of Bethesda.

The life I began to live through the water of baptism is a vital involvement in the mystery of Jesus, Son of God. Such participation in the life of the Lord should be manifested by the fruitfulness of my life as God's child. It means a life of vibrant

64

faithfulness, a life of works demonstrating and revealing to the world the Christ whose life I live.

Today's Prayer Focus

STAND UP AND WALK

Wednesday—Fourth Week of Lent

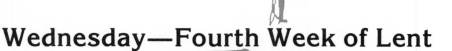

What Does God Say to Me Today?

(Let the following commentaries direct your reflections on today's scriptures.)

Isaiah 49:8-15

God summons his people to new greatness. The prophet compares their return from exile to repossess the land of God's covenant pledge to the passage of God's people in the Exodus. God shepherds them, once again protecting them and providing adequate food and water during their journey home. In one of the most touching descriptions of divine love to be found in the pages of scripture the love of God is compared to the love a mother has for a child. The existence and extent of God's love can never be fully grasped by the human mind.

Psalm 145:8-9, 13-14, 17-18

God is praised for faithfulness to his covenant oath to care for his people.

John 5:17-30

Jesus identifies himself as the Son of God, unique in being equal to the Father, sharing the divine nature of the Father and able to do the work of the Father. His work is to share the life he has eternally from the Father with people here and now. Those who listen to him will receive that life.

Today's Retreat Focus

I take for granted the unimagined reality that God has given me the life of heaven itself, the fact that I am his child. I take it for granted as I take for granted my mother's gift of life to me. Lent is a time for remembering!

God's love is a mystery of fidelity, far exceeding even the love of a mother for her child. I know from personal experience the depth and extent of a mother's love. In giving me life she gave me part of herself and then released me, permitting me to be independent and free. A mother's timeless love of her child involves understanding, patience, tender care, alertness, support, compassionate forgiveness, never-ending concern, clear and firm direction. If my mother's love has demonstrated anything to me it is that I am worth more than even I at times have suspected. If her love has taught me anything it is that I am forgivable.

God loves me that much and infinitely more. Today I confront and respond to the reality of that love. God my Father loves me because he sees Christ in me. He loves me as he loves his eternal Son, Jesus, whose life I share. Lent is a time for remembering!

Today's Prayer Focus

REMEMBER GOD'S LOVE

Thursday—Fourth Week of Lent

What Does God Say to Me Today?

(Let the following commentaries direct your reflections on today's scriptures.)

Exodus 32:7-14

God was grievously offended by the idolatrous worship of the golden calf by his people. Moses assumed the role of a mediator between God and his unfaithful people. Through his intercession God turned his wrath aside and reconfirmed his covenant pledge of faithfulness to his people.

Psalm 106:19-23

In hymn style the malice of idolatry is lamented. Today's song concludes on the note of God's pardon for the most malicious infidelities of his people.

John 5:31-47

In the first part of this gospel account, by means of different witnesses, Jesus defends and justifies his claim that he is the Son of the Father and does the works of his Father. In the second part he makes a summation and delivers an indictment against the Pharisees and religious leaders.

Today's Retreat Focus

Moses took a risk in assuming the role of an intercessor before the infinite God, but God responded positively to the pleas of the finite Moses. The Lord Jesus is the new Moses, a most powerful mediator, perfectly able to represent me because his divine person possesses both human and divine natures in his Incarnation.

He is on the level not only of the Father who is offended but also on the plane of humanity which has done the offending. He pleads for me through the ransom price of his own annihilation. Moses took a risk for God's people of old. Jesus took a risk for me. He is my mediator now according to my need at this moment of my existence.

Today's Prayer Focus

JESUS, MEDIATOR

Friday—Fourth Week of Lent

What Does God Say to Me Today?

(Let the following commentaries direct your reflections on today's scriptures.)

Wisdom 2:1, 12-22

The purpose of the Book of Wisdom was to strengthen the faith of a people being lured by pagan religions and secular philosophies of life. Today's text describes wicked men who hold in contempt the servant of God who is totally consecrated to doing God's will. Jesus will identify himself with that servant—tested, persecuted and condemned to a shameful death because his life and words are a reproach to those who have adopted pragmatic atheism as a way of life.

Psalm 34:17-21, 23

To possess wisdom is to be able to see things from God's point of view. To possess wisdom is to realize that God always responds to his people with concerned care, and to recognize that suffering is a part of life even for the just.

John 7: 1-2, 10, 25-30

Opposition to Christ becomes overt when he goes to Jerusalem for the feast of Tabernacles. That was the beginning of the final events of his ministry. Dismissed as the Messiah, the Lord emphatically declares that his enemies' knowledge of him is minimal and superficial, that he really can be known only when he is recognized as the One sent by God. Those who reject him don't know God and therefore are unable to recognize him. He can reveal God because he has come from God.

Today's Retreat Focus

The drama of Christ's rejection which will result in his crucifixion is now heightening in pace and intensity. I should experience increasing tempo within my own Lenten retreat experience. I have to make decisions about personal issues of faith response—selfishness, secret idolatries, ritualistic prayer and worship, my role as a child of the Father, my response to Christ in my neighbor's need, lack of trust in God, firm acceptance of God's pardon of my weaknesses and malice. The decisions to be made are specific. They demand a change in the very depths of my person. I hesitate and recoil from making them. I am as divided in my firm acceptance of Jesus as were the people in today's gospel. To do the will of my Father is the challenge confronting me. Total consecration to the will of God alone will also identify me as the Servant of God, the faithful child of the Father, the Christian.

Today's Prayer Focus

SERVANT OF GOD

Saturday—Fourth Week of Lent

What Does God Say to Me Today?

(Let the following commentaries direct your reflections on today's scriptures.)

Jeremiah 11:18-20

The prophet Jeremiah, the spokesman for God, learns of a conspiracy to murder him because of the indictment of idolatry he has leveled against the faithless people of God. He proclaims his innocence and puts his trust in God's care of him. Jeremiah here suggests the image of Isaiah's Suffering Servant of God, both of them standing as prophetic types fulfilled by the Lord Jesus. It should be noted that the strict justice of retaliation of the Old Law was abrogated by Jesus with his commandment of total forgiveness even of one's enemies.

Psalm 7:2-3, 9-12

Here is a song of lament by a person unjustly accused, pleading for God's help in his hour of need.

John 7:40-53

The evangelist once again records the division among the people about the messiahship of Jesus. The religious leaders are becoming desperate in their attempts to silence Jesus and contemptuously dismiss anyone who is attracted to him as being ignorant, unlearned in the Law. The Pharisees manifest their conviction that knowledge of the letter of the Law is more important than its observance. The confusion, the charges heard here and the organized power of the Pharisees are beginning to electrify the air, creating the atmosphere which will result in the death sentence for the Lord Jesus.

Today's Retreat Focus

The chief priests and Pharisees of Jesus' day were religious men. They followed a strict regimen of religious practices. They worked hard at it to the point where they held non-practitioners in contempt.

However, their ritual was detestable to Jesus. He showed them up as pious frauds practicing their own type of idolatry. Their self-righteousness, their blindness, took them to unimaginable lengths in their efforts to eliminate Jesus.

Today I confront the fraudulent in me.

A personal crisis normally results for the victim of unfaithfulness. It is terribly painful to be hurt and set aside, to be rejected by those I love, by those whom I have trusted or those I have helped in their time of need. Jesus experienced such rejection and so have I. The crisis of faith is not in ceasing to be faithful but in becoming a counterfeit, one who feigns faithfulness.

To be faithful essentially consists in giving oneself to those who have a right to take—my God and my neighbor. It is a life of being emptied of self and being filled with the Spirit of Jesus. That is the meaning and the process of putting on Christ, of becoming a person of faith. That process is the action of my Lenten retreat.

Today's Prayer Focus

CRISIS OF FAITH

Monday—Fifth Week of Lent

What Does God Say to Me Today?

(Let the following commentaries direct your reflections on today's scriptures.)

Daniel 13:1-9, 15-17, 19-30, 33-62

Daniel's rescue of the chaste Susanna is a folk tale. It is not a historical account. Several explanations are proposed of the purpose of the story: that with God's help virtue conquers vice, or that the two elders symbolized those who tried to lure the good into unfaithfulness to God.

Psalm 23:1-6

God's care of his people, especially in time of greatest need, is vividly described by the psalmist as that of a shepherd who protects, provides sustenance and sure guidance to his flock.

John 8:1-11

A sinner stands before the incarnate God and experiences his mercy. The Lord, in his practical way, challenges the woman's accusers to consider whether they are so free from sin that they are able to pass judgment and carry out the punishment of a fellow sinner.

Today's Retreat Focus

Today God directs his word to me personally. I know whether I am like Susanna or the woman of the gospel account. The reality to be experienced is that God compassionately cared for both of them although they were so different, one guilty and the other innocent. God's care was the same for both of them. Spared destruction, life was given to each of them.

The story of Susanna has application to the people who have a responsibility for others. I can be faithful or be a seducer in fulfilling such responsibility. Lent is the time to be recommitted to any responsibilities which are mine to lead or to form others in covenant fidelity. Lured by the secular philosophy of the day and the cultural standards of the times it is very easy to seduce by silence, example or instruction the very persons I am responsible to lead. This is an issue which leaders must consider seriously during this retreat.

Today's Prayer Focus

THE LORD IS MY SHEPHERD

Tuesday—Fifth Week of Lent

What Does God Say to Me Today?

(Let the following commentaries direct your reflections on today's scriptures.)

Numbers 21:4-9

Leading a semi-nomadic life during the 40 years between escape from Egyptian bondage and their entry into the land of God's promise, the people of God in their weariness, insecurity and terror frequently complained against their leader, Moses, as well as against their God. The incident recorded in this reading occurred at the time when people were fleeing from the threatening army of the Edomites. They refused to trust. Punished for their infidelity, they receive God's mercy. Punishment for sin is overshadowed by God's healing pardon. God heals, based on the people's faith in him.

80

Psalm 102:2-3, 16-21

In profound suffering the psalmist pleads for God's help. Recalling how God had always responded to the people of Zion he now pleads as a lone individual for that same response to his present personal need.

John 8:21-30

In this confrontation it is apparent that the Pharisees are absolutely unwilling to believe Jesus, that they are closed to the manifestation of the divine power of his works, and that they have totally rejected him as the Messiah. Jesus foretells his crucifixion and hints that his resurrection and ascension not only will proclaim the validity of what he has been telling them but even more will give witness of God's presence to them.

Today's Retreat Focus

Today God's word describes the conflict between two worlds. The pilgrim Israelites, wandering in the inhospitable wasteland of the Sinai, yearned for the comparative comfort and security of the world they had left behind in Egypt. There at least their basic needs were satisfied. In the gospel Jesus charges that the Pharisees are unable to understand him or have the faith which would permit them to accept the life he offers them because they have allowed themselves to be oriented by earthly values and secular standards. I must choose between a materialistic world and a world of faith. The two worlds cannot be blended to create a response to God which is personally palatable or convenient. This retreat is geared to analyze my faith response and make changes which become apparent.

Values, standards of conduct, priorities of life and religious practices are frequently a response of Christian culture rather than a response of faith. The way I approach and participate in the vital mysteries of redemption during Holy Week can be a valid measurement of my faith. Personal responses to those in need are too often humanistic rather than a response of love for Christ who suffers in my neighbor, my brother or sister. My worship often can be a search for novelty or mere fulfillment of ritual rather than an expression of personal faith.

There are so many issues which are woven like threads into the fabric of my faithfulness. Each of them must be examined and treated during this Lenten retreat.

Today's Prayer Focus

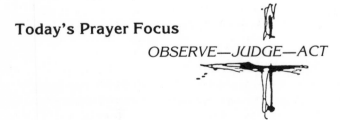

OBSERVE—JUDGE—ACT

Wednesday—Fifth Week of Lent

What Does God Say to Me Today?

(Let the following commentaries direct your reflections on today's scriptures.)

Daniel 3:14-20, 91-92, 95

This legendary tale of three faithful Israelites was directed to Jewish people living a century and a half before Christ whose commitment to continued faithfulness was challenged by a royal order to participate in pagan worship under threat of death. The message would dramatically remind them that God protects his people from harm when they are faithful to him.

Daniel 3: 52-56

Freed from any harm through divine intervention, the three condemned young Israelites prayerfully sing a song of praise to God.

John 8:31-42

Faith is not intellectual assent. Salvation is not obtained with mere external identification with a community of believers. Faith requires personal action based on professed beliefs. Jesus explains that the spirit of Abraham's trusting response to God must be found in anyone who professes to be a person of faith. The Lord announces to his audience that he is the Son of God, the final fulfillment of the promises made to Abraham, father of their race, and that he has come to give freedom to those who have faith in him.

Today's Retreat Focus

Today is a day of decision, a time to accept Jesus as my God. He has manifested himself to the world and to me. To accept Jesus as Lord demands my personal response to his gospel in the direction and context of life here and now. To respond to him with the faith of Abraham will release me from self and permit me to enjoy the freedom of a child of God.

It will be impossible to live a life of faith if I don't trust God. Like a child learning to walk who trusts in the caring and watchful presence of a parent, I have to trust God if I am going to walk free. Faith is trusting God.

Today's Prayer Focus

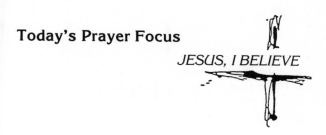

JESUS, I BELIEVE

Thursday—Fifth Week of Lent

What Does God Say to Me Today?

(Let the following commentaries direct your reflections on today's scriptures.)

Genesis 17:3-9

The covenant pledges made by God to Abram, father of the Hebrew people, are recorded in these few verses. Abram is portrayed with his face pressed to the earth, his posture professing positive acceptance of God's covenant terms. God changes Abram's name to Abraham, an act signifying the beginning of a new existence. Yahweh has committed himself to Abraham and his offspring.

Psalm 105:4-9

Worshippers are invited to join in praising God for his wondrous care of his people through the ages.

John 8:51-59

When Jesus proclaims his divinity he is immediately charged with blasphemy and the popular support needed by the Pharisees to carry out their evil plan is substantially increased. The movement toward the annihilation of the Lord gains momentum.

Today's Retreat Focus

The vivid picture of Abraham with face pressed to the earth was duplicated by the Lord as he lay prostrate in the Garden of Gethsemane in the acceptance of his Father's will. I shared that same experience on Ash Wednesday as my face was marked with ashes of the same earth as a sign of my response before the majesty of God and my intent during the progress of this Lenten retreat to cope with my personal faithfulness to God's revealed will to me.

Today's Prayer Focus

I AM

Friday—Fifth Week of Lent

What Does God Say to Me Today?

(Let the following commentaries direct your reflections on today's scriptures.)

Jeremiah 20:10-13

In the midst of persecution the prophet is torn by conflicting feelings of terror and trust—terror at the threats and attacks of his enemies, and trust that God will always protect him.

Psalm 18:2-7

A song of thanksgiving rises to God for his intervention which assures victory over the raging onslaughts of terrifying enemies.

John 10:31-42

Once again his enemies react in rage to Jesus' announcement of his divinity. This is the Lord's final lengthy

88

confrontation with them. Prejudiced and hard-hearted, they reject him. Concluding that they now have adequate evidence to convict him of blasphemy, they try unsuccessfully to arrest him.

Today's Retreat Focus

Good Friday is one week from today. The word of God in each of today's scripture readings begins to set the stage for the curtain about to be raised on the covenant drama of my redemption. Jesus is to be denounced, betrayed, terrorized and finally destroyed. He will be ridiculed and dehumanized. The Suffering Servant of God will experience physical, spiritual and emotional crises. The waves of death and the destroying floods, like a background rumble swelling in today's psalm hymn, will overwhelm Jesus.

My retreat task today cannot be limited to a surge of emotional pity for Jesus, the covenant victim, nor to a mere nod of intellectual recognition and acceptance of what was accomplished for me by the Lord. Today I must make a leap of faith, more absolute and unconditional than I have ever made before, accepting Jesus as my God and my redeemer. Unless I make that confession of faith as a retreat action today I should suspect that, unconsciously at least, I am judging him to be guilty of the indictment of blasphemy leveled against him by his enemies in today's gospel.

In their rage his enemies were brought to the point of stoning Jesus. That sight horrifies me. Yet I use stones of a kind against Jesus also. I can wall him off in my life by not having the faith to permit him presence in the circumstances and direction of my life. I can also wall him off by excluding people from my love and forgiveness or by not responding to his presence in my suffering neighbor.

Today's Prayer Focus

JESUS IS GOD

Saturday—Fifth Week of Lent

What Does God Say to Me Today?

(Let the following commentaries direct your reflections on today's scriptures.)

Ezekiel 37:21-28

The prophet foretells that in his goodness and compassion God will restore the people of Israel and Judah, now divided by exile, into his united people once again.

Jeremiah 31:10-13

The whole earth is invited to join in a joyful song of praise and gratitude to God for his redemption of his people, Israel.

John 11:45-57

The Sanhedrin, a council of 71 members permitted by the Roman authorities to control Hebrew religious matters, decides to eliminate Jesus. He is dividing the populace and upsetting the status quo to the point where the leaders fear that the Romans will decide to suppress all Temple worship. The council issues the order to arrest Jesus and the curtain rises on the drama of the passion and death of the Lord.

Today's Retreat Focus

God saves his people not because they are holy and good but because he is holy and good. The sequence of God's saving love is sin, punishment, redemption and repentance. Redemption comes before repentance. The prayerful consideration and grasp of such unimaginable divine love will provide the understanding and impetus needed to be an involved participant rather than a mere observer in the redeeming events to be renewed liturgically during the approaching Holy Week.

Today's Prayer Focus

SIN, PUNISHMENT, REDEMPTION AND REPENTANCE

Monday of Holy Week

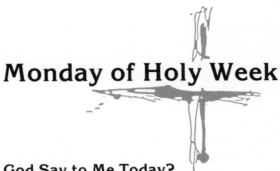

What Does God Say to Me Today?

(Let the following commentaries direct your reflections on today's scriptures.)

Isaiah 42:1-7

The first song of the Suffering Servant of God introduces this final week of Lenten retreat. The remaining Servant songs will be heard tomorrow, Wednesday and on Good Friday.

The Servant of God is the perfect Israelite, a person of absolute trust in God, completely consecrated to obedience to the will of God. He fulfills the role of king, prophet, judge and priest. The Servant is the powerful instrument of God who will reform humanity by an act as creative as the act of initial creation. A new creation will be accomplished by this chosen one, the Servant of God, through a new covenant, profoundly transforming people in the depths of their spirits.

Psalm 27:1-3, 13-14

A poem of trust in God is recited with this psalm prayer by an individual who faces complete destruction at the hands of evil men.

John 12:1-11

Lazarus, Mary and Martha, gathered with their guests at a dinner honoring Jesus, seem to have little realization of the hate which will result in his execution within the week. Mary's anointing of Jesus was extravagant, but it was an unconscious preparation for his burial. The haste to bury him following his crucifixion will not permit the anointing she now gives. His resurrection will make it not only impossible but unnecessary.

Today's Retreat Focus

Judas Iscariot objected to Mary's extravagance in using perfume which was valued at almost a full year's salary at that time. Some believers still raise the same objections. They believe that religion should consist of social action. The Lord responds that religion also has other claims.

The Servant of God came into the world gently and peacefully. He comes to me now in exactly the same way. "A bruised reed he shall not break, and a smoldering wick he shall

94

not quench." I am the reed bruised by past unfaithfulness and insecure about my future faith response. The battered, weak and bruised reed clings to life by tenuous fibers. The profound relationship of life in and with Jesus is frequently weak. Yet, the Servant of God is patient with me and accepts me as I am.

This Holy Week must not deteriorate into days of paralyzing anxiety because of memories of past unfaithfulness to God or insecurity about future fidelity. This week is a time for peace and confidence. The Servant of God comes to heal my wounds and strengthen me by his graceful presence.

Today's Prayer Focus

WAIT FOR THE LORD WITH COURAGE

Tuesday of Holy Week

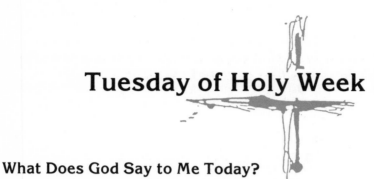

What Does God Say to Me Today?

(Let the following commentaries direct your reflections on today's scriptures.)

Isaiah 49:1-6

All the Servant of God songs were occasioned by the role which King Cyrus of Persia played in Jewish history. He liberated the Hebrew people from the Babylonian exile and permitted them to return to their homeland. Although initially viewed as the anointed one, his later actions as he established pagan temples and festivals in their holy city of Jerusalem showed that he was not the Messiah and that the true Servant of God was still awaited.

Today's song of the Servant of God describes his mission as embracing the Gentile nations as well as the Hebrew people. It should likewise be seen that the Servant described mysteriously refers not only to an individual person but the very community of God's people.

Psalm 71:1-6, 15, 17

The recollection of God's care in the past permits one to have confidence in his continued care in any future crisis.

John 13:21-33, 36, 38

The hour of darkness has arrived. The Lord identifies himself with the Servant of Yahweh suffering the results of the conspiracy of trusted friends. "It was night." The Light has shown in vain. The prophecy of Peter's denial is a prelude to the abandonment to be experienced by the Servant of God.

Today's Retreat Focus

There are three characters in today's gospel drama—Judas, Peter and Jesus. Each has a different value on life. For Judas, money is an idol, alone measuring the value even of a person's life. The meaning of life is unknown to him as will be witnessed in time with his own suicide.

Peter puts a value on life but measures it superficially. He will come to learn before the dawn of another day that his own life is his idol. He will protect himself once his life is threatened even remotely. His ego will fight with no thought to the cost of clinging to his life, a gift offered so boastfully in the safety of a dining room.

The Lord Jesus, the Servant of God, surrenders his life to friends and enemies. That surrender must be mine when, at the conclusion of this Lenten retreat, I commit myself to a life of covenant fidelity in the renewal of my baptismal vows

Today's Prayer Focus

SURRENDER

Wednesday of Holy Week

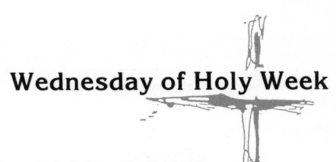

What Does God Say to Me Today?

(Let the following commentaries direct your reflections on today's scriptures.)

Isaiah 50:4-9

Supported only by his faith in God's continued care the Servant of Yahweh resigns himself to the suffering expected when the force of the storm of approaching persecution finally envelops him.

Psalm 69:8-10, 21-22, 31, 33-34

This psalm describes the suffering of an innocent man who relies solely on God to be spared.

Matthew 26:14-25

Judas Iscariot betrays the Lord Jesus for a sum of money equivalent to the value of a slave. At the paschal meal Jesus not only announces his betrayal but accepts it, deliberately yielding himself to it.

Today's Retreat Focus

With Jesus' announcement that one of their number would betray him, the apostles are curious about the identification of the betrayer. It is interesting that each of them questions his own loyalty to the Lord, thereby revealing anxiety about their personal loyalties to Jesus as well as their limited faith in him. Potential treachery exists in each of them and they are aware of it.

Sensing that same anxiety in the depths of my own spirit I prepare to renew fidelity to my baptismal vows at the close of this retreat. Although I can feel personal anxiety regarding future faithfulness I am aware at the same time of God's perfect patience with me and his pledge of ever-present merciful pardon.

The Servant hears God's word spoken to him through the suffering he is enduring. Because he listens, the Servant understands and accepts God's will. To do the will of God is to serve God and that alone is what matters. Suffering is God's creation and therefore has value. Only complete confidence in God permits suffering to be accepted. It is not merely tolerated but actually welcomed. Jesus understood this attitude toward suffering. He set in motion the events which will result in my sharing in the glorified life he brings from the empty tomb. Jesus took the initiative on my behalf.

For me to assume the Christian life is to assume the role and the title of Suffering Servant of God. Sanctity, essentially and ultimately, is my conformity of identification with Jesus in suffering. Confronting that issue prepares me to participate personally in the events of redemption to be renewed, continued and completed liturgically during the next three days.

Today's Prayer Focus

PUT ON THE LORD JESUS CHRIST

Holy Thursday

What Does God Say to Me Today?

(Let the following commentaries direct your reflections on today's scriptures.)

Exodus 12:1-8, 11-14

God provides detailed instructions regarding the meal to be prepared by the Israelites prior to their exodus from Egypt and the beginning of their journey to the land of God's covenant pledge to them. The blood of the slaughtered lamb is lifegiving. It will keep their families from being included in the final plague which God will send the Egyptians, the death of the first-born offspring, both human and animal.

Psalm 116:12-13, 15-18

Saved by God's care, the faithful servant, now fully aware of his value in God's eyes, sings a song of thanksgiving.

1 Corinthians 11:23-26

St. Paul reminds the Christians of Corinth that a covenant with God has been sealed for them with the blood of a sacrificial victim—Jesus himself. His redemptive death is proclaimed in the sacrifice of the Mass in which he is present until his final coming.

John 13:1-15

The Lord Jesus assumes the role of a slave at the Last Supper. By washing the feet of his disciples he exemplifies that love for others is fulfilled by humbly serving them. The Servant of God must serve others. To be his disciple demands the imitation of such a spirit. There is no other way.

Today's Retreat Focus

Jesus accepted his disciples just as they were, with feet of clay, and that is how he accepts me. Similarly, I must accept other people.

Jesus, at the beginning of his public ministry, was introduced by John the Baptist as the Lamb of God, the one fulfilling the sign of the paschal lamb which saved God's people of old. He is the unblemished Lamb who redeems the people, now sealing a new covenant with his own blood.

The paschal sacrifice, the Mass, never lets me forget what Jesus did for me. I lose the meaning of the Mass if I lose the meaning of sacrifice. The Mass is the offering of the sacrifice of Jesus for me to the point of his annihilation.

To complete the offering of the Mass must involve the whole Christ. Since I share his life I must be part of what's being offered. Only with that appreciation can I begin to offer Mass vitally, responsibly and fruitfully. I will be a mediocre Christian as long as my Mass is mediocre.

The annual ritual of the Passover meal required personal involvement of all participants by sharing in the meal. Eating the meal involved them in the mystery of the event of liberation being commemorated. My participation in redemption is completed in receiving the food of the Eucharist, sharing in a family, a fraternal meal.

Today's Prayer Focus

LAMB OF GOD

GOOD FRIDAY

What Does God Say to Me Today?

(Let the following commentaries direct your reflections on today's scriptures.)

Isaiah 52:13—53:12

This is the fourth and most important song of the Suffering Servant of Yahweh. The text is harsh and breathes apprehension and terror, suffering and death, yet is bursting with the assurance of liberation. It is a prophecy of the ultimate triumph of God's totally committed servant who, bearing the weight of others' sins, surrenders himself to horror and death which will result in redemption for the people.

Psalm 31:2,6 12-13, 15-16, 17, 25

Jesus uttered a verse from this prayer of trust as he hung on the cross: "Into your hands I commend my spirit," seeking the face, the presence of his Father.

105

Hebrews 4:14-16; 5: 7-9

Jesus alone can reconcile humanity to God. He has entered the Holy of Holies of God's presence as the great high priest eternally offering his perfect sacrifice of atonement.

John 18: 1-19, 42

John records the history of divine love in the account of the passion and death of the Servant of Yahweh who saves the people of God by the offering of himself to the point of annihilation as covenant victim.

Today's Retreat Focus

On this Friday called "Good" there should be profound peace and delight in the depths of my spirit rather than sorrow. This should not be a day of depression, of hopeless grief. There can be no heartbreak. There must be no tears.

Today I will be overwhelmed at the realization of the love of my Father in giving me his divine Son. Today I will be aware of the love of the Lord Jesus for me in offering himself as payment to the majesty and holiness of his Father, for the rebellion, self-will and infidelity of sin. Know the malice of sin which would need such a price tag.

The liturgy today is more than a drama performed on a stage. It is not play acting. It is not merely a story being told once again. It is the reality of my covenant with God my Father sealed by the personal involvement of his Incarnate Son. I am involved in the event of that passion and death and so am to be as active in them as is the Lord.

Today's Prayer Focus

BEHOLD THE WOOD OF THE CROSS
ON WHICH HUNG THE SAVIOR OF THE WORLD

Holy Saturday & Easter Sunday

How dark the world was for humanity when Jesus lay dead in a tomb! Today I try to grasp, to experience, the emptiness of a world without Christ. It's a dark void, an empty wasteland, without the presence of Jesus. I yearn for him to be present to me.

My world rings with the shout: "The tomb is empty!" The Lord has been raised up as he promised. The night is over. The paschal candle is the symbol of the risen Christ, the Light of the world, who pours the light of his presence into the dark corners of my being.

The saving work of the Lord began to be present to me in the dark water of the baptismal font in which I died to my personal drives and selfish wants. That was the reality of my sharing the tomb with Jesus. I shared in the resurrection event when I rose from the font now alive with the glorified life which the Lord brought from the empty tomb and still lives now in the presence

108

of his Father. This is the wonder I will celebrate in the Easter festival.

During the days of Lent I have answered the four basic questions of my existence:

Where have I come from?

Why am I here on earth?

Where am I going when I die?

How am I going to get there?

Now, having made the changes in my life demanded by the answers to these questions, I have come to the moment of renewing the solemn promises of my baptism when in accepting Jesus as Lord I likewise committed myself to obedience to the commandments of love of God and neighbor.

Renewal of Baptismal Promises

Renunciation of Sin

I reject sin, so as to live in the freedom of God's child.
I reject the glamor of evil and refuse to be mastered by sin.
I reject Satan, father of sin and prince of darkness.

Profession of Faith

I believe in God, the Father almighty, creator of heaven and earth!
I believe in Jesus Christ, his only Son, our Lord who was born of
    the Virgin Mary,
    was crucified, died, and was buried, rose from the dead,
    and is now seated at the right hand of the Father.
I believe in the Holy Spirit,
    the holy catholic church, the communion of saints,
    the forgiveness of sins, the resurrection of the body,
    and life everlasting.

God, all-powerful Father of the Lord Jesus Christ, has given me a
new birth by water and the Holy Spirit and forgiven all my sins.
May he also keep me faithful to my Lord Jesus Christ for ever and
ever. Amen.